LIVING SINGLE

Defining yourself...before someone does it for you!!!

By Lambert & Kim Sands

Copyright © 2014 Marriage Mechanics Ministries.

All rights reserved. No part of this book may be used or reproduced by any means, graphic, electronic, or mechanical, including photocopying, recording, taping or by any information storage retrieval system without the written permission of the publisher except in the case of brief quotations embodied in critical articles and reviews.

All Scriptures taken from the King James Version of the Bible.

Introduction

For most people, the grass always seems greener on the other side. Like the proverbial Catch 22, when we are tied to a partner, we want to be loosed, and when we are loosed, we yearn to be tied again. However, for some people singleness is not an option; it's their reality. Whether never married, divorced, separated, or widowed, they must embrace the pros and cons that come with the single lifestyle.

However, because of the misunderstanding of the purpose of being single, and the inability to live a single life of purity, few are able to harness the power of this lifestyle. God's purpose for singleness is preparation and strength so that we can be a blessing to someone else. *However, in these perilous times of selfishness, unthinkable arrogance, and sexual looseness, most single people have been spiritually crippled and deceived. They have little or nothing to offer those who come into their lives whether for marriage or simply friendship.*

The purpose of the book is spiritual illumination and guidance through the maze and darkness of our time. As always, our God has the answer, and his purpose for our lives is what we must embrace. Our singleness was never to make us lonely creatures, or desperately hoping for and seeking companionship. Nor was our singleness designed to make us solely creatures of pleasure. Our singleness was designed to *empower* us; to make us spiritually aware of our true purpose, and to make us *life coaches* for others. **"But he said unto them, All men cannot receive this saying, save they to whom it is given. For there are some eunuchs, which were so born from their mother's womb: and there are some eunuchs, which were made eunuchs of men: and <u>there be eunuchs, which have made themselves eunuchs for the kingdom of heaven's sake. He that is able to receive it, let him receive it.</u>" (Matthew 19:11-12)**

Lambert & Kim Sands

Table of Contents

Introduction..5

1. The Single Life..11
2. The Waiting Room - Loneliness..........................25
3. A Position of Virtue...31
4. Homosexuality - Spiritual AIDS..........................37
5. Now...I'm Really Angry!..44
6. A Little Bit About Drugs.......................................54
7. Money Matters For Singles..................................59
8. Bloom Where you are planted............................67
9. Single Maturity...73

1.
The Single Life

Daryl had been the senior pastor of Hunter's Creek House of Worship for nearly two years. A young bachelor, he had gone to college to study architecture, but midway through his studies found himself in a local church committing his life to God. When he graduated, he knew what he wanted to do. He wanted to preach the word of God. So taking his savings, and a desire to minister to wounded hearts, he built a strong and vibrant church in the heart of New York's inner city. However, little did he know that his greatest challenge would not be serving up passionate sermons, but cooling the flames of passion that sought to consume his mind and body.

During the first few months as senior pastor, Daryl was flattered by the amount of young women that surrounded him in church meetings. He was also surprised at the response he often received as he greeted many at the sanctuary door after the church service was over. Mothers would compliment him on his insightful sermon, and then add that they were praying that God would give him a good woman to help him in the ministry, while dropping subtle hints that their daughters were available.

This was all a part of the territory Daryl thought. This was until he met Jasmine. Jasmine was the girl that you met in your dreams and hated getting up the next morning. With short hair, sharp features and a body like a Victoria's Secret model, you had to take a second look. And, not to mention, she could sing like an angel.

She was from out-of-state and began attending church services after being invited by a co-worker. When Dave, his brother and choir director, learned that she had singing talent, he invited her to join the choir and eventually to be one of the lead singers. Daryl was excited to have a talented singer to uplift and energize the church during the Sunday morning services, but what would happen next would lead him down a dark alley that would be difficult to come out from.

It was Friday. Daryl usually left the office early but decided to stay a little longer to tidy up some paperwork. With the secretary gone, he was alone when he heard the voice of someone calling out, and asking if anyone was there. It was Jasmine. Daryl's heart fluttered. His office door was cracked opened, and he could see her. She was gorgeous. Dressed in silk slacks and a sleeveless blouse with a low cut that advertised her shapely bust line, she was the complete package.

He began feeling sensations he hadn't felt since he had become a Christian. Being single, he had his share of temptations with women in the church, but it was nothing like this. Walking toward his office, she continued to call out. She was looking for Dave, his brother who was the choir director.

"He is not here….he left around eleven!"

"Oh…Pastor Daryl…I didn't know you were here."

"Well, I'm supposed to be gone but I needed to get some paperwork done."

"Sorry to disturb you."

"No, no…it's okay come in."

When Jasmine came into his office, he could feel it. It was like electricity. They made eye contact, and the passionate heat evaporated every ounce of reservation he had. Daryl got up and walked over to close the door behind her. He just wanted to express his feelings to her…feelings he couldn't control. Before he could open his mouth, she grasped his hand and gently pressed it into hers. He could feel her eyes inviting him, and Daryl gave into the urge. He kissed her. The passion that he felt was intoxicating. His body was telling him to forget about everything he had ever heard about holiness and morality.

Seemingly in dream world, he felt when he let go. He grabbed her and lifted her into his arms. The clothes only took seconds to come off, and by the time it was finished, they were drenched in sweat and out of breath. He had never experienced anything like that. But, there was something else that he didn't bargain for: guilt.

Over the next several days, he tried to get it out of his mind. He felt the guilt but the passion and desire to see her again was overwhelming. He thought about what would happen if people found out. He thought about his relationship with God, but it was drowned out by the voice of passion that told him he had to see her again. He wanted her and nothing was going to stop him! He invited her to his apartment and again the steamy sexual interlude. After this, they met regularly; he was in love, lust, like…it didn't matter. Yes, he felt guilty and hypocritical, but the sexual passion was too much to deny. He had strayed off the path that he, as a minister, should be following and had lost his way.

When he preached, he could feel the shame within, and even more, when he looked at her in the first row of the choir seats. In his heart, he knew it was wrong but what could he do? Little did he know that he was not the only one captivated by Jasmine. So was Dave, his brother. Dave was under the same spell…only deeper.

Quiet and a bit slow when it came to words, Dave was nothing like his charismatic older brother. His passion was music, and being the choir director was a dream-come-true for him. So, when Jasmine came to service and displayed her singing talent, he felt energized, she was just what he was looking for to carry the choir to the next level.

He and Jasmine spent a lot of time together at rehearsals, and afterward they would go out to eat together. The conversations were very innocent usually revolving around making the choir better. Dave enjoyed being with the beautiful singer. He admired her, but was too timid to let her know how he really felt about her. Things would change after a Saturday afternoon practice.

Choir practice ended a bit later than expected and Dave and Jasmine were headed to their favorite restaurant, when Jasmine said she forgot something at her apartment and if they could stop on the way. When they got to the apartment complex, Dave was about to slump back in the car seat when Jasmine suggested that he come with her. At first, he resisted but when she said she wanted him to see her gospel collection CDs, he reluctantly agreed.

Dave strolled through the apartment door and made his way to the nearest sofa. Jasmine told him the CD collection was over on the table, and then excused herself to look for the items that she had left home by mistake. After a few minutes, she reappeared dressed in a very revealing negligée. Feeling heated and breathing heavily, Dave didn't know what to do...Jasmine showed him.

After a month of seeing Dave, Jasmine asked if they could go for marriage counseling so that they could get married. And, when he agreed, she revealed her secret sexual affair with Daryl. She blamed Daryl for it, and told Dave that she wanted to end it, but Daryl was unwilling to let go. This would be the bomb that blew up the Hunter's Creek House of Worship.

Dave approached Daryl, and it exploded into an intense argument with neither wanting to give her up. After six months of Jasmine attending the church, the love triangle had taken its toll. The gossip was intense, and church attendance took a sharp drop. There was also a growing call for Pastor Daryl's resignation.

Daryl was becoming desperate. He wanted Jasmine, but the cost was now bigger than he could pay. He was losing everything, and his life was now being defined by a love affair. He knew he had to do something, and one Sunday morning, instead of delivering another stirring message, he delivered his soul. He confessed before the congregation.

There were a lot of "Ooh"s and "Aah"s but he was free. He felt the sexual bondage break. Looking over to the choir section, he saw Jasmine walk out. It was finished. Now, he could go back to who he really was: A man of God!

> *"But thou, O man of God, flee these things; and follow after righteousness, godliness, faith, love, patience, meekness." (1 Timothy 6:11)*

> *"I say therefore to the unmarried and widows, It is good for them*

if they abide even as I." (I Corinthians 7:8)

"And the LORD God said, it is not good that the man should be alone; I will make him a help meet for him." (Genesis 2:18)

"But he said unto them, All men cannot receive this saying, save they to whom it is given. For there are some eunuchs, which were so born from their mother's womb: and there are some eunuchs, which were made eunuchs of men: and there be eunuchs, which have made themselves eunuchs for the kingdom of heaven's sake. <u>He that is able to receive it, let him receive it.</u>" (Matthew 19:11-12)

The above story illustrates the pitfalls of the single life. Singleness can be extremely rewarding as we use our free time to help others in our pathway. However, if we don't understand the mechanics of the single life, we can fall prey to the many deceptions and traps that the Devil brings to trip us up.

In the Old Testament, it seemed as if all the men and women of God were married, however, in the New Testament, the Apostle Paul admonished the Saints that being single was a better lifestyle. This appears to be contradictory; however, we can connect the two schools of thought, if we apply the wisdom of God. *If we don't, we will either find ourselves struggling with our flesh like celibate Priests who try to deny human nature, or we will resign ourselves to the belief that since there is so much lust in the world, marriage is our only option.*

Truth is, we were born single and our ultimate quest in life is to reunite and to be one with our Creator. However, although God created us as single human beings, we are created to be inter-dependent on our fellow man. We are to interact, form relationships, learn skills and enjoy life. This is why God said that it is not good that man should be alone and made him a partner.

We must remember, however, that before God created the second human being, Eve, he nurtured Adam's spirituality. He gave him chores and responsibilities e.g. dressing the garden, naming animals. All of this was done to train his spirit to flow in the wisdom and knowledge of God. He needed to achieve a level of spiritual maturity before he could have a partner. How profound!

This is the essence of the single life: to fortify our relationship with God; to understand our purpose; to become mature enough to interact with our spiritual environment, and with others. However, in our sexually charged world, we have been so bombarded with sexual advertisement in virtually every aspect of our daily lives, that few people ever develop their singleness. Instead of being able to help the other people in the lives, whether it's husband, wife, children, pastor, friends to a greater awareness of God and the purpose of life, we have become spiritual cripples, defined by our mistakes, unable to help ourselves, and unable to help anyone else for that matter.

Defining Oneself

Nobody would dream that behind Lambert Sands good-humored attitude lurked a shadowy character full of insecurities. Although I knew how to score with witty jokes and colorful sarcastic remarks about others, underneath my pseudo confidence, I was hiding my poor self-esteem and inner fears. That was my young single life, and I believe, without a doubt, it is also the life of most youths.

I entered a private Catholic high school, Saint Augustine's College in the Bahamas in 1974. This is where I developed character, made mistakes, went to detention, and grew to be a teenager. At this time in my life, I was indeed a ship without a rudder simply drifting with the wind. My mother was busy working two jobs frantically keeping bills paid, and too busy to give me quality time of instruction and coaching.

I was learning life from the corner boys and my best friend at school: a toxic combination. Without supervision and discipline I began to delve into a life of illicit sex and rebellion. This attitude cost me numerous detentions and several suspensions. My mother had no idea that her quiet son was busy living a double life. At home, I was very subdued; however, in school I was boisterous, lacked discipline and never backed down from a fight.

When I graduated high school I went to live with my father in the United States for a short time, but returned to the Bahamas when money ran out. Within a week, I had secured a job at Barclays Bank, a major banking institution in the Bahamas. However, my insecurities surfaced again. I hated most of my supervisors because they seemed so phony and pretentious. I rejected their authority and soon found myself on the verge of being fired.

After my one year probationary period, I got a terrible annual report that required another six months of probation. I was depressed. It was at this juncture in my life that Jesus Christ entered. After talking with a young missionary from the United States, I was hounded with conviction until I surrendered my heart to God.

After becoming a Christian, my life did a one hundred and eighty degree turn. The love that I felt for people and desire to serve overwhelmed me. My insecurities and cynicism gave way to genuine faith and love. Several years later, I was married to my wonderful wife Kim.

Under the guise of self-confidence and self-assurance, I made most of my mistakes in life. Without genuine faith in God, and without using the Bible as my road map, my insecurities made me a pawn in the hand of Devil to work mischief and deceit. You see, before we are able to properly interact with others, we must understand who we are. Why am I here? What should I be doing? What is my purpose? ***If we don't define ourselves, there is always someone who will define us.***

Like the teenager who runs away from home in rebellion to parental authority and ends up working as a prostitute for an abusive pimp, or the divorcee who runs from one marriage to the other hoping for love and validation of existence.

If we don't' acquire the skills and maturity that comes from a developed single person, we become susceptible to lies, confusion and the control by others who are likewise insecure and confused about their identity. Insecurity is fertile ground for the Devil and his imps to control the thoughts of an individual.

How many women and men would be better partners if they had been taught during their single years who they were according to the word of God? For example, a young man should be taught during his singleness the importance of sexual discipline, leadership, how to manage money, and how to interact properly with men and women.

If he has a good heart and embraces these lessons, he becomes sensitive to others; he avoids sexual activity and becomes a good steward of his resources. However, we know that all too often the opposite is true. Most young men engage in sexual pleasure before marriage; they party a lot, and usually avoid responsibility.

Some end up with illegitimate children who become a burden to their finances for life; others can not direct their families or properly relate to their wives, all because they never developed themselves during their single life. The same can be said of women who believe that life revolves around having a male to validate their existence. Having a boyfriend and exploring sexual fantasies take the place of learning how to properly care for a household.

Security

Your definition and calling will only come from a committed and focused lifestyle as you humbly obey God's word. Spend quality time in reading God's word and in prayer. Your talents and gifts both spiritual and natural must be explored and developed. This is best done when you are single and free from the burdens of marriage or other committed relationships.

Paul, the Apostle, told the young man Timothy to run from sexual temptation. *"Flee also youthful lusts: but follow righteousness, faith, charity, peace, with them that call on the Lord out of a pure heart." (2 Timothy 2:22)* He also admonished the young Pastor Titus to encourage young men to be "sober minded" (Titus 2:6). Indeed, it's easy when we are young and full of energy to believe that life will last forever. For many, fun and party takes the place of a serious and focused mindset; and living for the moment pre-empts thinking about the decisions that may affect us tomorrow.

However, if we simply slow down and collect ourselves, our vision becomes clearer. We can see through the lies of sexual temptation that never tell you about possibility of sexually transmitted diseases, pregnancies (some even chose to end the pregnancies with abortion); or worse, the emotional and spiritual wounds that cannot be cured with medicine or psychological therapy.

These satanic lies of sexual pleasure usually lead a lot of single people down a dark pathway of promiscuity where they lose direction and self-esteem. Many dreams and ambitions have been lost and delayed because of a lack of discipline during singleness. Many marriages suffer because of the mistakes made while being single.

When a woman or man delves in illicit sexual intercourse, they form soul ties with their sexual partners that are near impossible to break without the help of the Holy Spirit. So, when these individuals get married to someone else, when trouble comes, they sometime feel an inclination to get back together with their former sexual partners. This is another reason why a person should do their best to stay sexually pure while being single.

Kim's Experience

During my teenage years, I was almost daily bombarded with suggestions from my school peers to participate in premarital sex. "Kim, you don't know what you're missing." They claimed that it was enjoyable and the thing to do, however, I thank God for a strong family and church support that kept me from doing it.

Years later, these same friends confessed to me that they regretted that they participated in premarital sex. Like someone said, "The grass always looks greener on the other side of the fence." My chastity led to a better relationship with my husband and helped me to be a better example to younger people. It also eliminated a lot of youthful problems like: sexually transmitted diseases, emotional problems from broken relationships, and self-esteem problems.

I am grateful for my single years that taught me discipline and self-control. Now, even if my husband and I have differences, we can work through them without resorting to extra-marital affairs or even divorce. Through our relationship with God forged during those years of singleness, we can weather the storms of life that are sometimes brought by two hearts becoming one.

2.
The Waiting Room - Loneliness

The royal blue luxury car sped down the highway. Bishop Constantine Meyers was deep in thought, and almost missed the exit that led to his favorite place on Saturday morning. Happy that he caught the exit in time, he turned onto the road that led to a small coffee shop.

It was a place that he and his wife had frequented because of its close proximity to the highway and early opening hours. By the time he reached the waiting area, a long line had already formed. Tired from a sleepless night, he slowly slumped into a nearby sofa. He had gone to bed around 11.00 p.m. the night before, but sleep was not to be. He twisted and turned for hours, and the morning ride to the coffee shop was a welcomed relief. Almost forty miles from his home in Cleveland, Tennessee, it was the only way he could get away from the pain of loneliness.

"Bishop Meyers, where is your wife?"

He was half asleep when Peggy, the waitress, asked the question. He had drifted off thinking about how just five months ago, he and his wife were on their way back from a church conference and stopped by the coffee shop. Things were so different then. He wasn't a divorcee. He wondered how could he have let it happen? How? How could he have allowed, Marjorie, his wife of twenty-seven years to move out and file for a no-fault divorce?

She told him to make a life for himself because she was not coming back. Since then, time seemed to stand still. When he came home from the church office, he was greeted by the stillness of an empty house. There was no aroma of someone cooking coming from the kitchen. Instead, there was a pile of dishes, and leftovers from what he had eaten the night before. He had to call in a maid service to do the cleaning and ironing, but when the sun went down each evening there was no one to snuggle up next to him or share his pillow.

He had to get used to coming home to a quiet untidy home. No more home-cooked meals, and worse, no one to talk to or fuss with. He thought that this must be what hell feels like. After being married for so long, he had become accustomed to a life of companionship. He never truly understood loneliness until now.

Loneliness is not only physical; in fact, its deepest pains are emotional and spiritual. It is one of the deepest pain that mankind could ever experience. In the beginning of creation, God said, *"It is not good for the man to be alone,"* so he created a companion for him. (Genesis 2:18).

Loneliness is an emotion that is associated with feelings of desertion, isolation, and despair. These feelings can surround a person when they find themselves alone, without a friend or loved one. It is one of the most depressing experiences that humans can experience. When Jesus hung on the cross he experienced loneliness. There on that cold rugged cross, he cried out, "My God, why hast thou forsaken me?"

He uttered these words when his human nature felt the abandonment of God's Holy Spirit as he bore the sins of mankind. It hurt that others had turned their backs on him, but his hurt was made more pronounced when he could not sense the presence of God, his Father. Yet, this too was an experience that God wanted him to endure in order for him to be a compassionate and faithful High Priest.

If you are consumed by loneliness, whether through divorce or through the loss of friendship, remember Jesus felt it too. Your loneliness is a test. It is during these times of apparent loss that Satan viciously assails the mind. Attacks may come in the form of regret over mistakes that were made. They may come in the form of sexual temptation to ease the void or worse, thoughts of suicide to end the misery.

Remember, you mind is the battleground, and your only recourse is to daily submerge your mind in the word of God. It's the only way. The only way! With your spare time, and during times of loneliness, pour into the life of another the valuable experiences that you have learned. It may be a friend, children, a colleague at work and so on. As you give, you can expect God to give back to you.

Sometimes our loneliness is the by-product of our selfish lifestyle. We selfishly catered to ourselves, and lived only for our selfish desires, and then, it was given back to us. We overlooked the poor; we verbally abused sinners; we mistreated those who came to us for help. Now, we are alone and we need the help of others. However, even after our sins, and our apparent judgment, it is still not the time to give in to despair. Instead, it is God's opportunity for us to rescue our spiritual destiny. Help someone else; reach out! *(Isaiah 58:6-8)* *"Is not this the fast that I have chosen? To loose the bands of wickedness, to undo the heavy burdens, and to let the oppressed go free, and that ye break every yoke? Is it not to deal thy bread to the hungry, and that thou bring the poor that are cast out to thy house? when thou seest the naked, that thou cover him; and that thou hide not thyself from thine own flesh? Then shall thy light break forth as the morning, and thine health shall spring forth speedily: and thy righteousness shall go before thee; the glory of the LORD shall be thy rearward."*

Also, during our times of walking alone without friends, is always a time to build trust in God and build personal virtue. Sometimes, we are too close to our

3.
A Position of Virtue

"And beside this, giving all diligence, add to your faith virtue; and to virtue knowledge; And to knowledge temperance; and to temperance patience; and to patience godliness; And to godliness brotherly kindness; and to brotherly kindness charity. For if these things be in you, and abound, they make you that ye shall neither be barren nor unfruitful in the knowledge of our Lord Jesus Christ." (2 Peter 1:5-8)

"There hath no temptation taken you but such as is common to man: but God is faithful, who will not suffer you to be tempted above that ye are able; but will with the temptation also make a way to escape, that ye may be able to bear it". (1 Corinthians 10:13)

"But every man is tempted, when he is drawn away of his own lust, and enticed." (James 1:14)

It is everywhere you go, everywhere you look. Turn on the radio, and it can be heard in the lyrics of most songs. It is suggested in movies and TV programs. Even on many billboard advertisements, the suggestion is there. Sex. It is constantly put in our faces as the ultimate pleasurable experience.

A young single and close friend told me that because of sexual temptation, she is unable to sleep at night sometimes. Having experienced sexual intercourse before marriage and before becoming a Christian, she is now being tempted by the images that are being put in the front of her on a daily basis.

But what is the solution when you are single whether it's from broken marriage or never being married? The struggle to sustain a life of virtue has become a tremendous challenge in our time. But it can be done! We must always remember that God is always in control, and our quest in life is to unite with him; to follow and obey him.

We must begin our life of virtue by separating ourselves from ungodly associations. *"Be ye not unequally yoked together with unbelievers: for what fellowship hath righteousness with unrighteousness? and what communion hath*

Loneliness is an emotion that is associated with feelings of desertion, isolation, and despair. These feelings can surround a person when they find themselves alone, without a friend or loved one. It is one of the most depressing experiences that humans can experience. When Jesus hung on the cross he experienced loneliness. There on that cold rugged cross, he cried out, "My God, why hast thou forsaken me?"

He uttered these words when his human nature felt the abandonment of God's Holy Spirit as he bore the sins of mankind. It hurt that others had turned their backs on him, but his hurt was made more pronounced when he could not sense the presence of God, his Father. Yet, this too was an experience that God wanted him to endure in order for him to be a compassionate and faithful High Priest.

If you are consumed by loneliness, whether through divorce or through the loss of friendship, remember Jesus felt it too. Your loneliness is a test. It is during these times of apparent loss that Satan viciously assails the mind. Attacks may come in the form of regret over mistakes that were made. They may come in the form of sexual temptation to ease the void or worse, thoughts of suicide to end the misery.

Remember, you mind is the battleground, and your only recourse is to daily submerge your mind in the word of God. It's the only way. The only way! With your spare time, and during times of loneliness, pour into the life of another the valuable experiences that you have learned. It may be a friend, children, a colleague at work and so on. As you give, you can expect God to give back to you.

Sometimes our loneliness is the by-product of our selfish lifestyle. We selfishly catered to ourselves, and lived only for our selfish desires, and then, it was given back to us. We overlooked the poor; we verbally abused sinners; we mistreated those who came to us for help. Now, we are alone and we need the help of others. However, even after our sins, and our apparent judgment, it is still not the time to give in to despair. Instead, it is God's opportunity for us to rescue our spiritual destiny. Help someone else; reach out! (*Isaiah 58:6-8*) *"Is not this the fast that I have chosen? To loose the bands of wickedness, to undo the heavy burdens, and to let the oppressed go free, and that ye break every yoke? Is it not to deal thy bread to the hungry, and that thou bring the poor that are cast out to thy house? when thou seest the naked, that thou cover him; and that thou hide not thyself from thine own flesh? Then shall thy light break forth as the morning, and thine health shall spring forth speedily: and thy righteousness shall go before thee; the glory of the LORD shall be thy rearward."*

Also, during our times of walking alone without friends, is always a time to build trust in God and build personal virtue. Sometimes, we are too close to our friends and partners that we allow them to obscure our view of God. We value their opinion more that God's word; we trust them instead of seeking and trusting him. Thus, being the jealous lover that God is, he must remove these hindrances so that we can see him: our Lord and Master.

It is during these times of being alone, we get an unobstructed view of God; free from the contamination of someone else's opinions. This is what God wants for his people: that they would get to know Him. This is the purpose of your existence.

Patience
"In your patience possess ye your souls." (Luke 21:19)

Most mistakes in our lives are made because we lack patience. We live for the present and forget about the long term effects of our decisions. Like Adam and Eve, we want to be worshipped and appreciated but we forget that if we eat the fruit, we will die!

In your "single" time, patience is your ally. He is your friend. Many people after being single for a time are anxious for a relationship and many make grievous and foolish decisions by jumping into a passionate relationship, without considering the consequences.

Patience teaches you to observe; look before you leap; investigate, pray and talk it over. These are effective tools in keeping your heart from the hurt and pain that comes from bad relationships. Alas, most singles, whether they are separated divorced or widows hastily enter into relationships that they later regret.

Remember, God has a plan. We must humble ourselves and wait on him. He said, I will never leave you nor forsake you. We must trust that he knows what is best for us. The promise for those who wait is summed up in this scripture, *"But they that wait upon the LORD shall renew their strength; they shall mount up with wings as eagles; they shall run, and not be weary; and they shall walk, and not faint." (Isaiah 40:31) light with darkness? And what concord hath Christ with Belial? or what part hath he that believeth with an infidel? And what agreement hath the temple of God with idols? for ye are the temple of the living God; as God hath said, I will dwell in them, and walk in them; and I will be their God, and they shall be my people. Wherefore come out from among them, and be ye separate, saith the Lord, and touch not the unclean thing; and I will receive you, And will be a Father unto you, and ye shall be my sons and daughters, saith the Lord Almighty."* (1 Corinthian 6:14-18) *"Now we command you, brethren, in the name of our Lord Jesus Christ,* **that ye withdraw yourselves** *from every brother that walketh disorderly, and not after the tradition which he received of us."* (2 Thessalonians 3:6)

This is the first mistake that singles make that cause them their virtue, reputation and, sometimes, their future. They get too close for comfort. They are unaware that the boy, man, woman who is trying to befriend them, may actually be the Devil in disguise. Lacking spiritual awareness, they fall into the trap that the enemy sets for them.

At the beginning, everything seems perfectly innocent. And then, it happens! You find yourself kissing, touching, the fire starts, no one can put it out, and the whole house of virtue burns down. Our perilous times demand that we keep our spiritual awareness button to its highest point, and it's the only way that we will survive.

There was a time that it was appropriate to say "keep a safe distance from the opposite sex." However, I think it is most appropriate to say, "Know who you are dealing with at all times, whether male or female." Another friend (I will call her Christina) who is estranged from her husband told me that she had developed a friendship with a female co-worker and would drive her home after work.

Christina enjoyed the friendship but after several weeks of doing this, the co-worker told her that she felt like she was falling in love. Of course, Christina was shocked and quickly dissolved the friendship. This is an example of not being spiritually aware. Christina was unaware of the spiritual forces at work in her so-called innocent relationship.

Many singles have been caught up in lesbian, homosexual and promiscuous relationships right in church. Lured by someone who appeared to be spiritual or fellow Christian, they let down their spiritual guard and came under the spell of influence of sexual spirits that promise pleasure but bring much anguish and guilt that comes from living a hypocritical life.

The only way to avoid this lifestyle is: keep your distance. Sex is too alluring, deceptive and powerful for us if we get too close. Even some of the most spiritual people in the Bible were seduced by sexual temptation. Keep these two words in your vocabulary when sexual temptation approaches, "Retreat and run."

Building Virtue

After you have separated yourself, build virtue! This is the purpose for which you were created. We were not simply created as sexual beings whose sole focus is sexual intercourse. Our focus should always...always be: **His will.** *"Thy kingdom come...thy will be done..."* "Not every one that saith Lord, Lord shall enter the kingdom of God but he that doeth the will of my father in heaven." *(Matthew 7:21)* People will not go to heaven because they warm a bench every Sunday. They will not go to heaven because they are familiar with prominent Bible doctrines. Neither will they go because they are a member of a good denomination.

People will go to heaven because they did the will of God. So, if that is the truth, why don't we simply do his will? Why don't we pray and seek God's face until he reveals to us his purpose and perfect will for our lives? This sounds easy and indeed it is. The truth is however, most of us would rather delude ourselves into doing what we like rather than submitting to God's will.

Take for example, the simple command for children to obey their parents; simply respect and obey their parents. Yet, the vast majority of young people would find every reason why they shouldn't subject themselves to their parents. *"They're old and out-of-sync with our times, they're too strict....they're too...."* They justify their selfish and self-centered motives and actions. They disqualify themselves from God blessings, though lack of virtue and obedience to his will.

You see, the enemy knows where the blessing of God's word is. It's in obedience and submission. However, most people have been tricked and deluded into thinking that Christianity is about how they appear to others. As a result, few build virtue in their lives through a close relationship with the Lord.

The word of God must be obeyed. It must be our daily bread and lifestyle. This is the only way to overcome and surmount the trials and tribulations that come our way. Our trials and difficulties in life are not meant to make us bitter but to make us better as we learn to trust God even when things look bleak and hopeless.

4.
Homosexuality - Spiritual AIDS

During July 2013, national media organizations carried a breaking news story of the changing position of the Roman Catholic Church toward homosexuality. However, it was nothing more than an embellishment of impromptu and ill-advised remarks made by the Pope; it showcased the ambition and drive of the homosexual agenda to promote the acceptance of the vile and heinous sin of homosexuality throughout the world.

Without doubt, recently, there has been an avalanche of homosexual stories in the media. Many of the stories are exaggerations, misinformation, and sometimes very morbid and crude untruths meant to showcase homosexuality as a natural and viable lifestyle. People are told homosexuality can be found among various species of animals. So humans, being primates, are perfectly normal if they are homosexuals. Professional athletes are being reprimanded for inappropriate homosexual comments. Then, the wife of President of the United States, called a homosexual person to congratulate him for "coming out" or openly letting everyone know that he was a homosexual, and the list goes on.

Sadly, most people are not even aware of impact and the significance of this torrent of homosexual information passed on as being normal and innocuous. The media, especially in America and the UK, show a decided bias never allowing stories about the opposite point of view to be told or showcased (I guess it would be considered hate speech or some form of phobia). Thus, the avalanche continues unabated, with younger people and a new generation who have no fundamental religious upbringing or teaching, destined to accept and embrace homosexual doctrine. They are unsuspectingly being infected with the spiritual (HIV).

During the 1980s was our first encounter with the dreaded Human Immunodeficiency Virus (HIV) which struck first at the homosexual community. The virus immobilizes and destroys the human immune system. The resulting condition and disease is called **A**cquired **I**mmune **D**eficiency **S**yndrome (AIDS). The disease doesn't kill you; however, it leaves the body defenseless to the ravages of all other diseases including the common cold. People who contracted AIDS during the 1980s died quick and untimely deaths, causing much fear and trepidation among the homosexual community.

Similarly and spiritually, homosexuality has the appearance of toleration; live and let live; and we have a right as consenting adults to do whatever we desire; but it's a mirage and teaser for greater and more profound wickedness and debauchery which if left unchecked, will lead to the end of civilization. Just like HIV, this destructive and invasive sin threatens the very fabric of society.

Male and female represent the foundation of civilization. Males represent authority and responsibility. Females represent the essence of life, wisdom and creativity. And even though either one can sometime substitute when there is neglect or absence of the other, when males and females fulfill their awesome responsibilities, they produce a balanced seed of stable, responsible, and gender secure individuals. Indeed, it's spiritually and emotionally attractive to see a woman who is feminine, bashful, yet strong and secure. Similarly, a man who is responsible, leads his family, yet is humble and sensitive enough to listen to his wife's advice and accepts her equality.

Homosexuality is the anti-thesis and contradiction of this. If we recognize and accept a man pretending to be a woman or a woman pretending to be a man as normal, we then endorse Satan's greatest and most vile deception, because, isn't it a deception for someone to pretend to be something that they are not? Like Satan pretends to be God? If we accept homosexuality, a man having sexual relations with another man or a woman having sexual relations with another woman, then, what about polygamy; what about bestiality (apparently now on the rise), what about lowering the age of sexual consent; what about a man having sexual relations with his daughter, or a mother with her son; and the devilish list can go on? Evil then multiplies exponentially, thus, the "AIDS" effect of homosexuality. Wow!

My friend, homosexuality is not a new phenomenon. It's an old, very old perverse sin and spiritual disease that led to the utter destruction of Sodom and Gomorrah. This is true! This is real! This has happened! *"And turning the cities of Sodom and Gomorrha into ashes condemned them with an overthrow, making them an ensample unto those that after should live ungodly; And delivered just Lot, vexed with the filthy conversation of the wicked: (For that righteous man dwelling among them, in seeing and hearing, vexed his righteous soul from day to day with their unlawful deeds;)" (2 Peter 2:6-8)*

We, the human race, are known for this one thing: repeating mistakes! We love doing the same things over and over again hoping for a different result. We get smart; we invent stuff; we feel enlightened; we have money; then, we become prideful and stupid. *"Professing themselves to be wise, they became fools, ...For this cause God gave them up unto vile affections: for even their women did change the natural use into that which is against nature: And likewise also the men, leaving the natural use of the woman, burned in their lust one toward another; men with men working that which is unseemly, and receiving in themselves that recompence of their error which was meet. And even as they did not like to retain God in their knowledge, God gave them over to a reprobate mind, to do those things which are not convenient;" (Romans 1:26-28)*

Then, God has to step in and clean it all up like Sodom and Gomorrah and in Noah's time. *"And as it was in the days of Noe, so shall it be also in the days of the Son of man. They did eat, they drank, they married wives, they were given in marriage, until the day that Noe entered into the ark, and the flood came, and destroyed them all."* (Luke 17:26-27) *"Likewise also as it was in the days of Lot; they did eat, they drank, they bought, they sold, they planted, they builded; But the same day that Lot went out of Sodom it rained fire and brimstone from heaven, and destroyed them all. Even thus shall it be in the day when the Son of man is revealed."* (Luke 17:28-30)

Homosexuality signals judgment! We are headed toward judgment with-I may add-speed! The Lord continues to warn us, especially the spiritual leaders in America and the western world who love to point fingers at the government to create a smokescreen for their own lack of motivation to evangelize. You see, if there is no revival, and the Church of the Lord Jesus Christ does not travail in prayer and revival, the Lord himself will judge. This generation will not pass away until everything is fulfilled. That means dire judgment!!! Remember Sodom and Gomorrah! Remember Noah! Lot waited until it was too late before running around like a chicken with his head chopped off telling everyone about the impending doom. The present church is no different. Living lavishly in the present world, we are that Laodicea church, rich in goods and believe we have need of nothing. (Revelations 3:14-22) Yet, we are divorced, lazy, without real evangelism, and spiritually asleep. God help us!!

We, the born-again Christians, are the light of the world. We are the salt of the earth. We have a job to tell our neighbors about the Living Christ and the God who can save any one. We are to share God's message of salvation and love with the world. Whereas, many homosexuals are reprobate, there are still some who are hurting, bruised and confused. They need someone to shine the light of God's mercy and love to them.

This reminds me of a young man who was a homosexual that worked at a large department store where I live. When we visited the store, he seemed to flaunt his homosexual behavior. He would toss his hips and act real feminine and the like. One day, my wife witnessed to him telling him about the love of Jesus and praying with him. About two weeks later, when I visited the store, he ran up to me to tell me about his new found relationship with Jesus Christ. He was simply ecstatic! He didn't have religion, no; he had a real relationship with the man called Christ! He recounted to me how he found Christ and his new devotion to witnessing and telling others about Christ. God is still in the saving business…let's get busy and put a stop to the AIDS disease!

5.

Now...I'm Really Angry!

When it happened, it felt like I was watching someone else in a movie. I had jumped to my feet in front of the classroom and pushed my math teacher's hands away from me and said, *"What's wrong with you woman!"* You could hear a pin drop in the ensuing silence; everyone was caught off-guard by my loud outburst. The math teacher was trying to discipline me for some remarks I had made with an ear cuff. I was having none of it, and stood up to her.

The assistant principal, who was making his afternoon campus walk rounds, quickly ran into the class and grabbed me. He started to carry me to the Dean's office. Again, I was hostile and pulled away from him. The anger had consumed me, and I was not thinking straight. Finally, I relented and was carried to the Dean's office. By that time, I was thinking straight and was horrified by my behavior. But it was too late; the damage had already been done. Fortunately, I wasn't suspended but was given detention instead, after sobbing for an hour blaming the incident on "no lunch" and insensitive treatment by my callous and snobbish math teacher.

Before I became a Christian at nineteen, I had many more of these out of control anger outbursts and several afterward. It wasn't until I learned forgiveness and true humility that I got the "beast" under control. You see, we usually blame our anger problems on people and circumstances rather that look at the man in the mirror. It is easier to blame others or circumstances than come to grips with the truth.

For me, my anger problems started with the hurt and pain of knowing that my father would not be there for me. Whether it was money or an event, he never helped or showed up. Divorced, my mother was the bread winner for four boys including me. I was unaware of the resentment and hatred that began to build up in my young heart. Coupled with this, as I grew older, I met other guys who were also dealing with the same issues, and gravitated toward their angry and destructive attitudes.

It was a formula for uncontrollable anger; anger that if left unchecked and unregulated leads to violence and destruction. I am grateful that God didn't allow it to get to the point where I physically harmed someone. However, it did cause me problems on my first job and early problems within my marriage. Anyone who has uncontrollable anger is a hostage and servant of that pent up anger.

However, we need not despair. The answer is finding the root and digging it up. As I related, my initial problems at the root of my anger was unforgiveness or the need to punish someone for a perceived wrong. I didn't forgive my father for his absence in my life, and I was unconsciously holding other people responsible for his actions. Even after becoming a Christian, I unknowingly still held on to these deep-rooted feelings that caused issues in my relationships with others.

For some people, the cause may be past abuse. Someone abused them physically or sexually and they never confronted the situation with a view to resolve or reconcile, and as a result the emotional wounds festered. They are unaware that their existing thoughts, reactions, and choices are influenced by the past experiences.

It's hard to see this at times, however, if we really dig deep, and in the right spot, we can find the poisonous roots that prevent us from healing and reconciliation. Much of the violence that we see in the world today is a direct result of someone or a group of people holding on to old grudges and grievances. We internalize the wrongs done to us, and bury them deep within our hearts. As a consequence, our minds and thoughts become hate-filled and distorted. We can never have a proper and open relationship with another, and our only recourse is true forgiveness.

Forgiveness means we release people and the past hurt, real or perceived, that others may have inflicted on us. We let it go! We pray for them. We bless them. We heap love on them if need be. This is the only way to wholeness and healing. Scripture says *"But if ye do not forgive neither will your Father which is in heaven forgive your trespasses." (Mark 11:26)* Remember, holding on to past grievances is like drinking poison and hoping the other person dies. It never works.

Willful Pride

"Only by pride cometh contention: but with the well advised is wisdom." (Proverbs 13:10)

"Proud and haughty scorner is his name, who dealeth in proud wrath." (Proverbs 21:24)

"In the mouth of the foolish is a rod of pride: but the lips of

the wise shall preserve them." (Proverbs 14:3)

Akin to unforgiveness is the need to ***always*** have one's way *(you must have your way regardless of being right/wrong or consequences)* whether in conversation or actions. This is called willful pride. We are so absorbed by own thoughts and conceited behavior that we ignore the need to hear and give others equal opportunity to explain or defend their actions. It's what we believe, and what we think, regardless of what circumstances are or what others put forward. Willful behavior is at its least very dangerous, and at its worst, very destructive as we run roughshod over others. With this attitude, we alienate ourselves by emotionally and spiritually bruising people sometimes without even knowing it.

This type of pride begins with the worship of ourselves. We think that we are very intelligent and of course, a very good person. So, how dare others not bow to our assertions and wishes? They must know that we are right, and listen and obey. This delusional way of thinking and acting leads to arguments and unnecessary confrontations with others.

The antidote for pride is genuine humility; the humility that comes when we recognize our own unworthiness and the need for God's grace and wisdom. For some people, this may seem to impinge on their self-esteem and self-worth. However, remember, problems in life result from our disobedience of the two most important commandments: Loving God with all our hearts and minds, and loving our neighbors as ourselves. When we neglect and disobey these two commandants, we invariably reap the consequences of this disobedience which are: a toxic prideful attitude and bad relationships with others.

Selfish and self-centered, we become agents of destruction as we hurt and abuse others with our callous behavior. We become our own god, and with our willful behavior, we are insensitive to others, and display to the world our immaturity and spiritual shortcoming.

The Good Anger

When God placed the emotion of anger in man's psyche, it was a good thing. ***God designed anger as a very strong emotion to confront, prevent, resist and overcome evil.*** This emotion is a demonstration of God's mind toward evil: He hates it! In fact, scripture describes God as a man of war. *"The Lord is a man of war the Lord is his name." (Exodus 15:3)* Anger is the propelling agent for us to fight evil. Properly regulated in the human's psyche, anger is meant to resist and overcome danger both physical and spiritual. Excellent examples of this can be found in the Bible's narrative of the lives of King Saul and our Lord Jesus Christ.

> *"And, behold, Saul came after the herd out of the field; and Saul said, What aileth the people that they weep? And they told him the tidings of the men of Jabesh, <u>And the Spirit of God came upon Saul when he heard those tidings, and his anger was kindled greatly.</u> And he took a yoke of oxen, and hewed them in pieces, and sent them throughout all the coasts of Israel by the hands of messengers, sayings Whosoever cometh not forth after Saul and after Samuel so shall it be done unto his oxen, And the fear of the Lord fell on the people, and they came out with one consent." (1 Samuel 11:5-7)*

> *"And the Jews' Passover was at hand, and Jesus went up*

> *to Jerusalem, And found in the temple those that sold oxen and sheep and doves, and the changers of money sitting: And when he had made a scourge of small cords,; he drove them all out of the temple, and the sheep, and the oxen; and poured out the changers' money, and overthrew the tables; and said unto them that sold doves, "Take these things hence; make not my Father's house an house of merchandise." And his disciples remembered that it was written, The zeal of thine house hath eaten me up." (John 2:13-17)*

In each case, we can see that anger was a demonstration of God's will. In the first example, God wanted Saul to conquer Israel's enemies. In the second example, Jesus' anger was a result of the blatant misuse and defilement of the sanctity of God's temple. In neither case was there uncontrollable venting of personal animosity and ill feelings. This is the big difference between good anger and bad anger. One is vented because of our selfish flesh, pride and the desire for control over others, while the other is displayed under the guidance of the Holy Spirit and the desire for righteousness.

When a person is displaying his anger under the guidance of the Holy Spirit, he can indeed *"be angry and sin not." (Ephesians 4:26)* His flesh is not active and influencing his actions. On the other hand, if a person's anger is controlled by his flesh and a need to dominate others, abuse, whether verbal or physical can take place. Anger is a very strong emotion and the Bible strictly admonishes that one should not be hasty to be angry. *"Be not hasty in thy spirit to be angry: for anger resteth in the bosom of fools." (Ecclesiastes 7:9) "Cease from anger, and forsake wrath: fret not thyself in any wise to do evil." (Psalm 37:8) "He that is slow to anger is better than the mighty; and he that ruleth his spirit than the that taketh a city." (Proverbs 16:32)*

There are times in all of our lives when the need to display anger is necessary. There are times when I have seen the poor overlooked and disregarded by the community and churches and it makes me angry. When the word of God is misinterpreted and used to bring God's people into bondage instead of liberty, a fire of anger ignites in my spirit. There are times when my wife has done things contrary to sound judgment or set down rules that have made me angry.

I believe that this is the type of anger that we should have. In fact, I wish the whole church would get angry with the Devil and pray until the demons of cancer, oppression in every form, and poverty are totally vanquished from the church and the earth. **We need anger that motivates us for justice and righteousness.** All the great men in history who fought for justice and righteousness were motivated by this *good* anger.

6.
A Little Bit About Drugs

"Wine is a mocker, strong drink is raging: and whosoever is deceived thereby is not wise." (Proverbs 20:1)

"It is not for kings, O Lemuel, it is not for kings to drink wine; nor for princes strong drink. Lest they drink, and forget the law, and pervert the judgment of any of the afflicted. Give strong drink unto him that is ready to perish, and wine unto those that be of heavy hearts." (Proverbs 31:4-6)

"Let him drink, and forget his poverty, and remember his misery no more." (Proverbs 31:7)

"And be not drunk with wine, wherein is excess; but be filled with the Spirit. Speaking to yourselves in psalms and hymns and spiritual songs, singing and making melody in your heart to the Lord" (Ephesians 5:18-19)

I wanted to fit in. I wanted to be tough like the other guys in my neighborhood, so at age fifteen, I started smoking cigarettes. It only lasted two weeks, and after reading a public service announcement at a movie theater that said you can get lung cancer from smoking, fear gripped me, and I quit. That was my experience with drugs. God was merciful to me and pulled me back before I ventured further. And, although I may have never moved up the ladder to marijuana or cocaine, the introduction to drugs is always the same.

We need to have peace. My insecurities and my desire to fit in was the catalyst for using a drug: nicotine (the drug in cigarettes). However, whether it's alcohol, cocaine, marijuana, heroin, nicotine or some other mind-altering drug; all drugs have one purpose: create another atmosphere or mind disposition. Mankind needs to have peace and stability. We want to have power and control over our reality; and when we can't, some of us resort to reinventing our reality with drugs. The "high" that we experience is our power over reality and the problems that we face. It's an illusion, and the reason people spend enormous amounts of money for the upkeep of their false reality.

For all of us, life has ups and downs; successes and failures. Whether in our personal relationships with family and friends or with our finances and health, there is always something going on. That is life, and none of us will escape it. For some people, like me, it may be the need to feel included and be a part of a group. For older people, it may be the need to feel secure and stable after the loss of a loved one.

For others, it may be the need to move beyond their poverty and have financial success. For some, it's a bad relationship and the list goes on. Drugs provide us with a way of escape and a pseudo sense of power over our circumstances, but, it's nothing more than a self-induced deception. When drugs are abused, time, money, self-respect, and relationships are all wasted and damaged. The very thing that we hope to achieve is destroyed and taken away from us. Wow!

Our fears, insecurities and pride propel us to take matters into our own hands. We want to fit in; we want to get rid of the emotional pain that we feel inside; we want to cover-up our mistakes and shortcomings of the past and present. Drugs become the choice for many who don't know how to face their fears and search for true and genuine healing.

The key to fighting addiction is dealing with your issues. Issues fester in our lives because we hide and cover-up because of our fear, insecurities and pride. We simply struggle with being real and genuine. To be real and genuine mean we have to admit to mistakes and shortcomings. We have deal with the rape or molestation. We have to come to grips with our abusive childhood; deal with a neighborhood overcome by gangs; or with a college campus of rich kids and your family is poor.

Of course, confronting our fears and insecurities is never easy. They have gained a foothold in our psyche and sometimes disguise themselves as legitimate attributes of our character and personality. We call our fears: concern. We say that our anger issues are a necessary protection against those who want to harm us. We refuse to deal with our molestation and abuse issues because of the problems and upheaval it would cause within our families. So, the misery goes on. We conclude that drugs are the best way to cope and have peace and stability.

The mountain is too high to climb, so we end up destroying ourselves. But, there is a much better way. It's called humility and patience. It's called repentance and forgiveness. God loves you and has a plan. He said, *"For I know the thoughts that I think toward you, saith the LORD, thoughts of peace, and not of evil, to give you an expected end. " (Jeremiah 29:11)* Begin your journey to healing by forgiving yourself. Pride and self-loathing says, "It's your fault…you should have known better." Humility says, *"But God commendeth his love toward us, in that, while we were yet sinners, Christ died for us." (Romans 5:8)*

God loves you right where you are. Life happens to all us. Some of us were born into very abusive families. Some of us will be molested by a family member. Some of us will make stupid, costly mistakes, and choices. Other times, it's sickness and disease.

But, the answer is not in a bottle of alcohol or shooting up heroin. The answer is not crack cocaine. They are delusions and false temporary feelings of peace and tranquility. The answer is Jesus.

Peace comes from the Lord who said, *"Peace I leave with you, my peace I give unto you: not as the world giveth, give I unto you. Let not your heart be troubled, neither let it be afraid." (John 14:27)* Anything else is an illusion.

Drugs are a demonic means of control and domination over our lives. Promising peace and control, but it does everything else. Many people have lost friends, acquaintances, and family loyalty as they lied, stole, and manipulated others to feed their addiction. After each use, it gains greater influence and control over our psyche creating a dependence and addiction that is hard to break. It's never worth it. The irony of drug use is that the very thing that people try to attain with drugs always eludes them.

Those who choose the Lord finally get the peace and tranquility that they yearned for. The Lord will never disappoint us. If you have never used drugs, keep away. If you are fighting the battle to stay clean or trying to overcome addition, surrender your life to the Lord. He has the power to take away the addiction and desire for drugs. He has the power to keep you clean. Reach out in faith and experience His power and graciousness.

7.
Money Matters For Singles

When I got my first month's paycheck from Barclays Bank, I felt like I had gotten a million dollars. It was a little over five hundred dollars; however, after working summer jobs as a student making a meager income, this was a lot of money to be paid all at once. I immediately went on a spending spree buying new television equipment, and clothing for myself.

I wasn't a Christian at this time, so, most of what I did revolved around me. Although I wasn't really careless about my spending, I was naive to the true value and use of money. Anyone, who doesn't have a good understanding of the value of money, will be either enthralled by the power and prestige, or fall prey to nagging problems that abound with people who don't know how to manage their wealth.

This concept proved true for me when my mother became ill and passed away and I had to learn money management. Without a budget and effective money management plan, I was always coming up broke. Coupled with that, I failed to listen to the voice of wisdom that came from my office manager and others who offered advice on pertinent money issues.

You see, when it comes to money and the issues of life, wisdom is always the principal thing. (Proverbs 4:7) Always. God is ultimately in control, and we need to carefully filter the voices in our mind, and those that come from without, for the wisdom of God, or, life becomes hard.

> *"But thou shall remembereth the Lord thy God; for it is he that giveth thee power to get wealth, that he may establish his covenant which he sware unto thy fathers, as it is this day." (Deuteronomy 8:18)*

> *"Honor the Lord with thy substance, and with the first fruits of all thine increase: So shall thy barns be filled with plenty, and thy presses shall burst out with new wine. (Proverbs 2:9-10)*

> *"Will a man rob God? Yet ye have robbed me. But ye say, Wherein have we robbed thee? In tithes and offerings. Ye are cursed with a curse; for ye have robbed me, even this whole nation. Bring ye all the tithes into the storehouse, that there may be meat in mine house, and*

prove me now herewith, saith the Lord of host, if I will not open you the windows of heaven, and pour you out a blessing, that there shall not be room enough to receive it. And I will rebuke the devourer for your sakes, and he shall not destroy the fruits of your ground; neither shall our vine cast her fruit before the time in the field, saith the Lord of host. And all nations shall call you blessed; for ye shall be a delightsome land, saith the Lord of host." (Malachi 3:8-12)

"But this I say, He which soweth sparingly shall reap also sparingly; and he which soweth bountifully shall reap also bountifully. Every man according as he purposeth in his heart, so let him give; not grudgingly, or of necessity; for God loveth a cheerful giver." (2 Corinthians 9:6-7)

"Give and it shall be given unto you good measure, press down and shaken together and running over shall men give unto

thy bosom. For with the same measure that ye mete withal it shall be measured to you again." (Luke 6:38)

"He becometh poor that dealeth with a slack hand; but the hand of the diligent maketh rich." (Proverbs 10:4)

"Be thou diligent to know the state of thy flocks, and look well to thy herds." (Proverbs 27:24)

"For wisdom is a defence, and money is a defence: but the excellency of knowledge is, that wisdom giveth life to them that have it. (Ecclesiastes 7:12)

"Much food is in the tillage of the poor; but there is that is destroyed for want of judgment." (Proverbs 14:23)

"He that loveth pleasure shall be a poor man: he that loveth wine and oil shall not be rich." (Proverbs 21:17)

"He also that is slothful in his work is brother to him that is a great waster." (Proverbs 18:9)

As long as we are upon this earth, and until the Lord comes, we must remember that money is our means of upkeep. The wise man Solomon puts it this way, *"A feast is made for laughter, and wine maketh merry: but __money answereth all things__." (Ecclesiastes 10:19)* So, when God puts money in our hand, we need to know what to do, especially as a single person. Without a second voice of authority, it's just us, God, and our resources.

Firstly, when God gives us money, he expects us to honor and recognize the person who gave it. This is called tithing and giving. We should take a tenth of our income and deposit it in the house of God, along with other monetary gifts. Then, we must pay those whom we owe because of services and goods we have purchased: light, water, telephone, grocery, etc. Then, we should consider those who are in need. Then, comes savings, investment, and pleasure! This is what budgeting and money management is all about. We think before we spend.

When you have put your budget and money management in place, then, in a practical way, learn to dominate money, this is the key to financial prosperity. Never allow money to dominate you. Develop habits of budgeting and thriftiness. Develop habits of maximizing income and minimizing expenses. Listen to the Spirit of God as he gives wisdom and direction while shopping or spending. Pay attention to household expenses to ensure conservation and prudence.

Try to conserve as must as possible, but don't be a slave driver or Scrooge about it. Being practical and thrifty is not an end. It's a means to saving money, so, being critical and frugal can be very unnerving and highly distasteful in a marriage relationship. So, as a single person, be firm with your finances, but sensitive and kind when dealing with others; willing to give and help others when necessary.

Learning to do some repairs and maintenance work yourself is a good way to conserve. God can give you wisdom to be a handyman or handywoman! This can cut down enormously on the household budget. For example, the house needs painting or the car may need a tune-up. Don't wait until the walls of your home become an eyesore before you react or the car stalls on a major highway. Be proactive instead of reactionary, look for wear and tear and fix and maintain as needed. The Bible says, that the way of the slothful is as a hedge of thorns but the way of the just is plain.

A passive mindset is the recipe for financial failure. The Devil can wreak havoc on your finances if you are not diligent. Debt can roll in on many different trolleys: parking or speeding ticket, unpaid bills, spending too much at grocery store, not watching the usage of electricity and water. However, being alert and financially conscious, you can avoid a lot of unnecessary financial hardships. It is also good preparation for living with a husband or wife.

Giving

This is very important principle that is often lacking among people because of corrupt organizations and deceptive practices of many who call themselves ministers. As a result, many people's trust has destroyed, and they are unable to reap the many bountiful financial and spiritual harvests that God intends for His people. We must remember that when we do give, we do it all in the name of the Lord. We give because of our faith and belief in God.

Of course, we should be selective in our giving. We should not give to an organization or people who will use our money, God's money, for ungodly purposes e.g. drugs, sex, build up a personal financial empire and the like. We want to put our money into good ground; we want to help people who are genuinely in need, and ministries that are doing the work of the Lord.

And, when we give, we can expect God to give back to us according to his word. It may not come the day after we have put fifty dollars in the offering or after our tithes envelope was collected, but it will come. God's timing is different from ours. While we are looking through imperfect faith and a dark glass, God in His sovereignty knows exactly when to let the blessing flow. Many people become frustrated when

God doesn't show up when they expect him. However, I am learning to relax, let go, and let God. Prosperity will come!

Wisdom means that we must always be open to the voice of God and be flexible when he wants us to change the routine a little. For example, I had just taken my tithe money from my bank account to carry to church on Sunday. I was walking out to lunch, when I met a Christian brother who I had not seen for almost a year. The Holy Spirit said, "give him fifty dollars." Some people would immediately start rebuking the Devil. But what was more important, a brother in desperate need, or carrying the tithe to church on Sunday. Yes, God wants us to be obedient in our tithing but I am sure He is much more concerned about the brother in desperate need. One need was more urgent that the other. This is true faith and obedience; flowing in the Spirit of God! A year later, that same brother related to me how God had really met his need that day.

Remember, money management is very important. Those who neglect this important principle will suffer unnecessary hardships and setbacks. Also, they will not reap the many bountiful harvests that God intends for his people. However, to be successful, we have to employ the principles of both diligence and faith. This means while we monitoring our finances, we are also spiritually alert to the guidance and wisdom of the Holy Spirit.

8.
Bloom Where You're Planted

The rain water slowly drizzled down the front windshield of Dana's car seemingly in a race with the tear drops that made their way down her cheeks. "Oh get going!" Dana said angrily to the woman in the car in front of her. She was frustrated and angry. Here she was on her way back from another wedding. This time, it was that of her twenty-one year old niece, Kathy. It seemed everybody in the world was getting married, or was already married. As the tears cascaded down her face Dana cried out, "Lord, will my day ever come?"

When it wasn't weddings, it was baby showers, anniversary or engagement parties. Dana felt she was never the focus, just one of the attendees with the most expensive gift. She began to wonder if that was why she was always invited. Nonetheless, she always found it exciting when she had to buy a present; it gave her an opportunity to pretend that she was actually buying the item for herself. She would pick the nicest things, because these were the things that she desired to own someday. Again she cried out, only this time in a whisper, "Lord, please hurry up with some spice for my life." Immediately she heard the response in her spirit, "Bloom where you are planted."

It has been said that the grass is always greener on the other side of the fence. However, many have come to realize also that what looks like green grass from afar can sometimes be weed. Many people look at the lives and material gain of others and pine away wishing that it belonged to them, or that they were in the other person's shoes. Millions of people watch Hollywood stars with all the glamour, fame, and fortune and aspire to one day have it too. They secretly long to live that life. Few stop to examine the reports of broken lives, misery, and pain that these people experience on an everyday basis, because life does not exist in the abundance of things.

In Mark 8:36 the question is asked, *"What shall it profit a man to gain the whole world and lose his soul, or what shall a man give in exchange for his soul?"* In the book of Revelations 3:17, we read of the Laodicean Church, a people that claimed to be rich, increased with good and in need of nothing. But the message to them from the Lord was that they were wretched, miserable, poor, blind, and naked. What a contrast! What would you give in exchange for the things that your heart desires? Will it be a lover that fits your fantasy? Or, will it be a big wedding, large sums of money, or a great career and fame? What will you trade for the life you think will make you happy?

Paul told the Corinthians to be content in whatsoever state you find yourself. As you look at your life, it might not look attractive or exciting. You would like to have more, but will more really satisfy you? *"But godliness with contentment is great gain." (1 Timothy 6:6)* In the day that we understand and accept this, we will be more at peace in our hearts.

Before you got to this point in your life, God knew what would be your destiny. He could have created you awesomely beautiful, super intelligent, and married with children, or filthy rich. He could have made you famous, or planted you in another continent to grow up in, but he saw that the ideal place for you would be right where you are today.

Maybe, you would have gotten married and bore two beautiful children, like a young woman in Texas, who believed she had the perfect family until she caught her husband in an affair and in heat of passion killed him. She is now spending her life behind bars. Or you might have been born in another state, married with no children, but living in misery. Who knows what your fate in life could have been. We will never know, but we have now, and we have today. Maybe you would have ended up dreaming of the life you have now.

Trust God to order your steps, and resist the suggestions of the enemy to desire what you do not have. Look at the flowers that bloom in the noon day sun, they cannot move or walk about from garden to garden, nor can they speak their mind, but they are happy to have rain and sunshine with every new day. The Lord said, *"For I know the thoughts that I think toward you, saith the LORD, thoughts of peace, and not of evil, to give you an expected end." (Jeremiah 29:11)*

One song writer penned these words,
Just a closer walk with thee,
Grant it Jesus is my plea
Daily walking close to thee,
Let it be, dear Lord, let it be.

God has your life in the palm of his hand. Trust him to lead and guide you. Make yourself available to him. Serve him and seek to serve others. As God continues to place the pieces of the puzzle of your life into place, you will be grateful, happy, and at peace in your soul. You are his original masterpiece. There is no one like you anywhere in the world. There might be someone who might look like you, or even share your name, but the truth is that God made only one of you.

For this reason, your life can never be like someone else's. What worked for Paul, or Peter will not work perfectly with you. Arise, shine, and allow God to perfect the being that he has made to bear his likeness and his glory. Take your position and bloom where you are planted.

What should I do….in the main time? This is a very common question from those that are unmarried, and waiting. At some point of living single every unmarried person will cry out, "What should I do in the main time? My answer to you is, "Live your life!" Too many singles wither away waiting for someone to come into their lives and sweep them away. Others become bitter and even blame themselves for allowing the college or high school sweetheart to get away. Some individuals get angry thinking that it is all their faults for not making better decisions, and all too often we meet those that continue to look in every crack and corner for that perfect person.

On the other hand some singles feel as if they have to settle for someone, anyone, because time is passing by. This is how many end up with a life of regrets. When we do what is right in our own sight, we often pay the greater price. We settle for silver not realizing that the gold was on its way. But there is only one way to make such a major decision and that is with much prayer. ***In your waiting, secure your soul.***

In the main time, the world is waiting for you, and the gifts and talents that God has given you are waiting to be used. Join a travel group, or create one yourself and enjoy the opportunity of seeing the world. Start a business, ask the Lord to give you an invention, or simply enrich the lives of those around you through being a volunteer or mentor to someone else. These are the very things that most married persons often don't have time for. Take every opportunity to venture a little.

First and foremost is your spiritual life which lays a foundation for you as an individual. A single person with a strong relationship with God will be strong enough to handle the major issues that come with a marriage when and if they decide to exchange vows. Your mannerism, your individuality, is one of the first things that beautify your character. A person's character, belief, and personal issues are magnified in a marriage relationship. Therefore, the well-rounded single increases the chances for a well-rounded person after the vows are taken.

Blooming where you're planted is the essence of the single lifestyle as we embrace God's will of our lives. Our challenges become lifetime trophies and our moments of loneliness become precious times of meditation and reflections that foster spiritual and individual growth. The grass may seem greener on the other side until our eyes are open to the luscious lawn that is under our feet!

9.
Single Maturity

Marla walked out of the courthouse. Smiling and jovial, she hugged her mother and sister who had come to provide support during her divorce proceedings.

> *"I am so happy this is over, Oh my Lord, now I can begin to live, I feel like I just got released from a cage!"*

Marla had only been married for a year but the marriage was now ended. It had been twelve months of hell. From the emotional abuse to the constant cheating, she felt drained. Now, it was over. She was single again, and now, how would she live her life?

Walking slowly through the parking area, she reflected on what had happened over the last twelve months of her marriage. Ed was as handsome and as charming as they came. When they first met, she felt that it was a "God thing". It was her thirty-fifth birthday and she decided to celebrate by going out to dinner at local restaurant. She loved the food and the entertainment and sitting at the table nearby was the most adorable man she had ever met.

Ed's charming demeanor was mesmerizing. His soft baritone voice put her at complete ease as he voiced his opinions on various subjects. When she excused herself to go to the restroom, he politely pulled out her chair. Her heart was captured. He was the man for her. This began their courtship that ended on a beautiful September morning when she stood at the front of Melonview Baptist Church to give her hand in marriage.

But only a month after the marriage, she found that she was not the only woman who found him exceptionally charming. The mysterious phone calls never ended and his whereabouts were always in question. When she approached him, he became violent and verbally abusive. The soft-spoken gentle teddy bear suddenly turned into vile snake spewing out deadly venom. Daily, he used abusive and demeaning words to destroy her self-worth and self-esteem. Her heaven became hell overnight.

But it was the explicit text message that drove her to the divorce court. The messenger detailed the sordid sexual experience that she and Ed had shared, and the desire to do it again. Marla felt has if she was being ripped apart, and the only way to feel secure and whole again was to divorce Ed.

Pulling the car door closed, Marla burst into tears. How could she have been so naïve and foolish? Are all men like this? What was her next step? A myriad of questions was pounding away at her mind. Her heart was bursting with emotion. She was free from Ed, or so she believed, but the pain that she felt was unbearable.

Sad to say, this is perhaps the roller coaster life of many singles today. In and out of relationships that bring only pain and suffering. They believe that their destiny lies in the arms of another. We see it in the popular magazines of the rich and famous, and in lives of our family and friends. They have been blinded to the truth. Your ultimate quest is not passion; it's a relationship with God.

While Kim and I were doing a marriage conference, Kim explained to the couples that marriage was for life, and there were no back doors. Of course, this created a stir. In the audience were a number of divorcees who vehemently disagreed with the doctrine of one husband and one wife until death. It didn't matter how their marriages had ended, or were consummated, they wanted to be married again.

With the large number amount of broken marriages, and toxic relationships, one would think that people would be cautious and treasure their singleness. However, the opposite is true. People are hoodwinked into thinking that another relationship of passion and sexual pleasure is the key to happiness and fulfillment. Or that companionship would heal the pain that they feel inside. What a deception and delusion!!

Whether we are married or single, our peace and happiness comes from our relationship with God. *"These things I have spoken unto you, <u>that in me ye might have peace</u>. In the world ye shall have tribulation: but be of good cheer; I have* *overcome the world". (John 16:33)* You can never get peace and happiness from people, it can only come from God.

This is the maturity and mindset that you must embrace. When people get married, they assume that their commitment to their marriage is contingent on the whether the marriage works or not. Like in the above story, as soon as the marriage went south, Marla headed for the divorce court. She lacked the maturity, fortitude and faith to give God a chance. Her choices and decisions were always dependant on someone else rather than the word of God.

Why did she marry Ed? He was a cool dude. Did she pray about it? Did she fast about it? Did she investigate his background? Oh Noooo…! Mr. Sugar and Spice was just right for her! She didn't need God or anyone else for that matter to tell her or advise her about marriage; the passion she felt was enough.

Now that she is paying the price, she got a divorce and maybe she will find her "God-man" the next time. Yea…right! For people who make these types of choices, the next time usually is worse. Until they look in the mirror and see the truth, they will continue this trend of hit and miss.

What is single maturity? It's about us. We must look in the mirror and analyze the decisions that we make and live with them. Whether you're single, or divorced, it was never about the other person. It was always about you and your relationship with God. **That is where the answer is.**

I got a divorce because Harry was a cheater. I got a divorce because Lucinda is a difficult woman to live with. No, you got a divorce because you failed to put God first. You failed to put him first when you were choosing a mate. And, then when trouble surfaced after you got married, you failed to put him first again. Sharp and pungent, but it's the truth!

Does this mean that when we put God first our troubles will disappear? No. But, it does mean that wisdom will be available when we are making our choices and decisions. It means that we will have the comfort of the Holy Spirit in our tribulations and problems. Yes, the power of the universe is available to those who will stay focused: put God first!! *"But seek ye first the kingdom of God, and his righteousness; and all these things shall be added unto you."* (Matthew 6:33) Putting his kingdom and righteousness first means it's not a democracy. The king rules! No questions! You simply obey the king.

We must always remember that our relationship with God must come before everything and everyone. God must be first in our lives. **His word must be the definition of who we are and guide the decisions that we make.** No "ifs" and or "buts". This is the pathway and the only way to living a successful single life.

It is not easy. We will be attacked by sexual temptation. We will be plagued by loneliness. We will be assailed with insecurity and fear, but we must hang on and wait until our change comes. The sweetness of heaven then and the peace of his Holy Spirit now are worth more than the sex and lies that Satan puts in the front of us.

Our maturity comes as we learn to live for the Lord. Obeying him daily as we embrace our singleness and our singleness of purpose: To please him. Then, and only then, will our peace and contentment become more abundant and complete.

About Us

Lambert and Kim Sands are ministers of hope and encouragement to marriages and relationships through a ministry called Marriage Mechanics. They have been married for more than twenty-seven years, and have been in ministry for almost thirty-five years. They have three children. The couple, originally from the Bahamas, presently lives in Deltona, Florida. Lambert and Kim reach out to the hearts of others with a word that is open, honest and Biblical. They are gifted speakers, and the authors of numerous books. They are also the hosts of Marriage Mechanics TV program. Their ministry reaches out to build the family, community, church, and ultimately the nations.

For more information write to:

Marriage Mechanics Ministries
2061 Watersedge Dr.
Deltona, FL. 32738

Ph. 407 385 8201

Email: marriagemechanics@hotmail.com

Other Books Available:

Her Feminine Side
The Real Truth *About* Marriage, Divorce & Remarriage
The Price of Dominion
I'm in Charge…Right?
Understanding Why We Fuss & Fight
Victory in the Bedroom
Cancer Doesn't Scare Me Anymore
Overcoming Jezebel, Delilah, and Anger
Fight For Your Marriage
The Treasure Box (Devotional)
Lord, Send a Revival!
The Noah Chronicles

www.ingramcontent.com/pod-product-compliance
Lightning Source LLC
Chambersburg PA
CBHW072104290426
44110CB00014B/1827